DISCOVERING DINOSAURS

ICHTHYOSAURUS

To J. G. B.

"*Thank you*" *to Dr. Nicholas Hotton III, Associate Curator of Fossil Reptiles and Amphibians, of the United States National Museum, the Smithsonian Institution, for reading the manuscript and for making helpful suggestions.*

BRONTOSAURUS

TYRANNOSAURU

Copyright © 1960 by Glenn O. Blough.
All Rights Reserved. No part of this publication may be reproduced, stored in a retrieval system, or transmitted, in any form or by any means, electronic, mechanical, photocopying, recording, or otherwise, without the prior written permission of the publisher.
Library of Congress Catalog Card Number: 60-8020
Printed in the United States of America
American Education Publications Paperback Book Club Edition
Published by Arrangement with
McGraw-Hill Book Company

PTERANODON

DISCOVERING DINOSAURS

by **GLENN O. BLOUGH**
PICTURES BY GUSTAV SCHROTTER

American Education Publications / A Xerox Company
Middletown, Connecticut

When you tell somebody that something happened a long time ago, you may mean that it happened a few years ago or before you were born or even before your father was born. But in this book when we write about dinosaurs that lived a long time ago we mean that they lived a LONG, LONG, LONG time ago. That means long before your father was born and even long before your grandfather was born or your great great grandfather. Long before there were any towns. Before there were books. Before there were people. Before

there was anything that you can see from your window now—except clouds and sky. And that *is* a very long time.

Dinosaurs lived on the earth millions and millions of years before there were any people. They lived on the earth about 170 million years ago. That was millions and millions of years before even the cave men lived on the earth. Nobody ever went dinosaur hunting because there wasn't any person living on the earth to go. So of course nobody ever met a live dinosaur in the woods or anywhere else.

Dinosaurs lived on the earth for a LONG, LONG, LONG time. They lived for millions and millions of years. They lived in many parts of the earth. Many of them lived in the part of the earth that is now the United States—in Wyoming, Colorado, Utah, Arizona, Texas, Montana, and in many, many other states. Of course, there was no United States then.

Dinosaurs ruled the animal world when they lived, millions of years ago. Some of them were the biggest of all animals. They were the fiercest animals. And there were more dinosaurs than any other kind of four-footed animals.

In those days there were no horses, no cows, no sheep, no squirrels. There were no birds. There were frogs and toads, but they were not like the ones we have today. There were fish in the sea, but they were not like our bass and trout. There were big sea turtles. Even though there were other animals on land and in the sea, those days of long ago were the days of the dinosaurs.

SEA TURTLE

Even the trees and other plants did not look then as they do now. There were trees and bushes that looked like palms and evergreens, but there were no oaks and maples. There were no garden flowers and no vegetables and no fruit trees. The animals and plants were very different then from the animals and plants that you see when you walk in the woods and fields. Dinosaurs lived in a very different world from ours.

What did a dinosaur look like? That's like asking, "What does a bird look like?" It depends upon what kind of a bird you are asking about. There are many kinds of birds. For example, there are owls and bluebirds and ostriches. But bluebirds don't look like owls and owls don't look like ostriches. But bluebirds, owls and ostriches are all birds. There were many kinds of dinosaurs too. And they didn't look alike any more than birds do. There were thousands of kinds of dinosaurs. You will be surprised at some of them.

Dinosaurs are all dead. They have been dead for millions and millions of years, but we know many things about them. We know what they looked like. We know what they ate, how they lived, and we know what happened to them. First let's look at some of these dinosaurs and see what they were like. We will just look at some of the biggest ones.

STRUTHIOMIMUS

PLESIOSAURUS

WHAT WERE DINOSAURS LIKE?

Dinosaurs were all sizes and shapes. Some were terrible giant animals that could look over a house and see what was in the back yard. But of course there were no houses and no back yards in the days of the dinosaurs. Some of them were the biggest land animals that have ever lived on the earth. Some were as small as the alley cat that can scramble under your back yard fence. And some were middle-sized, like sheep or pigs. Some were a little larger, about the size of horses and cows. Some were still a little larger, about the size of elephants. Many of them were bigger than you can believe. You can't tell what dinosaurs were like in one sentence, or even in two.

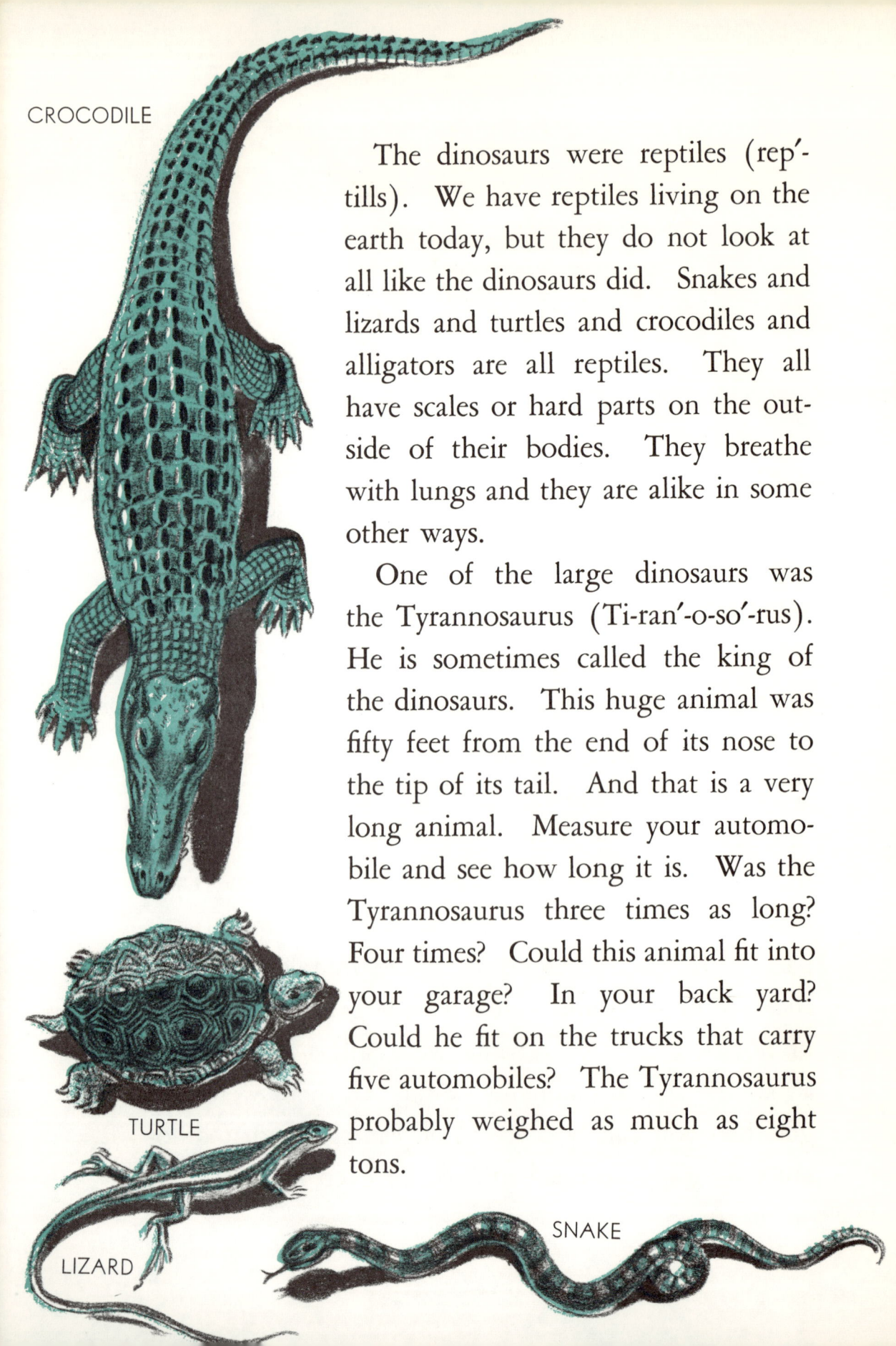

CROCODILE

TURTLE

LIZARD

SNAKE

The dinosaurs were reptiles (rep'-tills). We have reptiles living on the earth today, but they do not look at all like the dinosaurs did. Snakes and lizards and turtles and crocodiles and alligators are all reptiles. They all have scales or hard parts on the outside of their bodies. They breathe with lungs and they are alike in some other ways.

One of the large dinosaurs was the Tyrannosaurus (Ti-ran'-o-so'-rus). He is sometimes called the king of the dinosaurs. This huge animal was fifty feet from the end of its nose to the tip of its tail. And that is a very long animal. Measure your automobile and see how long it is. Was the Tyrannosaurus three times as long? Four times? Could this animal fit into your garage? In your back yard? Could he fit on the trucks that carry five automobiles? The Tyrannosaurus probably weighed as much as eight tons.

TYRANNOSAURUS

You see by his picture here that he had long, strong hind legs and small front ones. Many of the dinosaurs were built like this. When Tyrannosaurus stood on his hind legs and raised his head it was about twenty feet above the ground. Could he

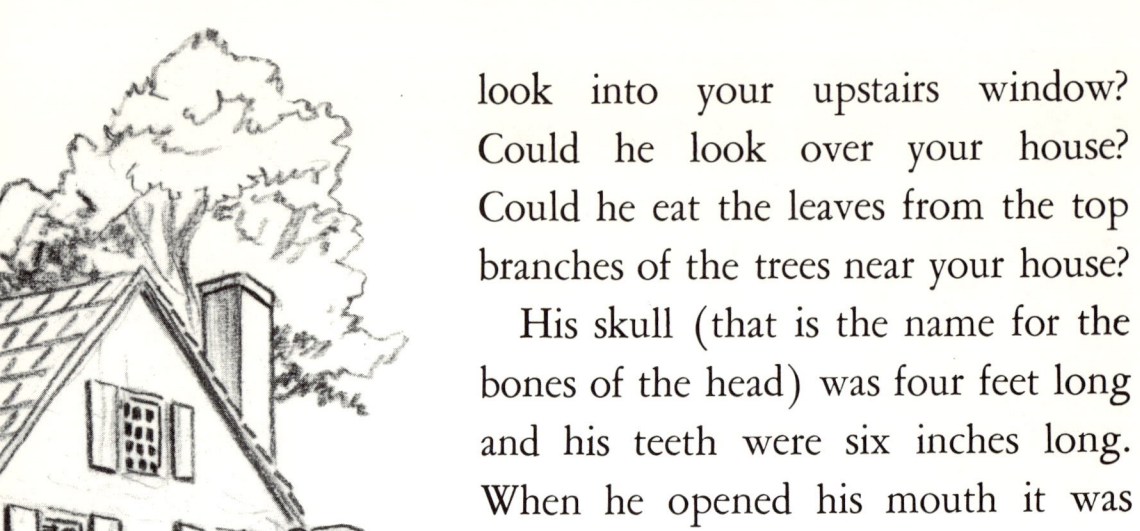

look into your upstairs window? Could he look over your house? Could he eat the leaves from the top branches of the trees near your house?

His skull (that is the name for the bones of the head) was four feet long and his teeth were six inches long. When he opened his mouth it was more than three feet wide.

Another of the large dinosaurs was Allosaurus (Al'-o-so'-rus). He grew to be as long as thirty-five feet. He had strong hind legs with strong muscles and large bones. He needed strong legs and muscles and bones because he was a very heavy animal. It takes strong bones and big muscles to move a heavy animal from one place to another.

Allosaurus walked on his big hind legs. His front legs were much smaller, and they had sharp claws that he could use to tear another animal into bits. And he did. Allosaurus didn't bother eating leaves and twigs. He ate only other animals.

ALLOSAURUS

Another huge dinosaur was named Brontosaurus (Bron'-to-so'-rus). That means "thunder lizard." The Brontosaurus weighed as much as thirty-five tons! He could shake the earth like a big truck going past your house or like loud thunder. No wonder he has been named "thunder lizard"!

Brontosaurus was as large as a half dozen elephants put together. Because of his huge size, he spent much of his time in shallow water. The water helped to hold up his large body.

Brontosaurus grew to be nearly seventy feet long. Could he get into your schoolroom? Could he turn around on your playground? You wouldn't want to be there on the playground with him because he was quite fierce to look at. He was not a meat-eating dinosaur. He ate plants, but he must have had to eat a lot of them to keep such a large body alive and moving.

BRONTOSAURUS

One of the fiercest looking of all the dinosaurs has been named Stegosaurus (Steg'-o-so'rus). What can you discover about Stegosaurus by looking at the picture? The plates that grew along the animal's back made him look fierce. They protected him. See the big spikes near the tail? He may have switched his spiked tail at his enemies. Can you imagine what happened if he did? Stegosaurus walked on all four feet. He was fifteen feet long and eight feet high. But he had a small head and a very small brain in it.

STEGOSAURUS

Many dinosaurs spent much of their time roaming over the land looking for something to eat. Some ate smaller animals. Some of the large dinosaurs ate smaller dinosaurs, and some of the large ones killed and ate each other. Some ate plants of all kinds, and others were both plant eaters and animal eaters, and still others were only meat eaters.

The big ones lumbered along like old tired elephants as they looked for animals and plants to eat. The little ones could run fast as a deer, and probably did, as they chased other animals for supper or went from one place to another to find new plants to eat.

TRACHODON, duck-billed dinosaur

Some dinosaurs spent much of their time in swamps or in the water. They found food there because the animals and plants they liked to eat lived there. Some kinds of dinosaurs got away from their enemies by hurrying into the water when enemies were after them.

Many of the dinosaurs walked on two strong hind legs. As you see in the pictures, their hind legs were longer than their front legs. Their hind legs were good for walking and their front legs for grabbing and holding food. There were long strong claws on their hind legs and on their front legs too. These claws were used to catch and hold and tear their food.

Many of the dinosaurs had strong teeth. Some had teeth for meat eating but more of them had plant-eating teeth. Can you tell what an animal eats by looking at its teeth? Look at your dog's teeth and you will see that he has sharp teeth for biting and tearing meat. Some of his teeth help him to hold on to his food. Some of them help to grind meat and get it ready for him to swallow.

If you have ever seen a squirrel's teeth, you know that he has strong teeth for eating nuts and other hard food. His back teeth are for chewing. Squirrels are plant eaters.

Your own teeth are good for eating both plants and meat. The front ones are for biting. The back ones are for chewing. Feel of them with your tongue and you can tell how they are different from each other.

Look at the pictures of the dinosaurs in this book and see if you can tell which animals were plant eaters and which were animal eaters.

We have told you about only a few of the largest of these animals. There were many other exciting ones.

Jaw of Allosaurus
(meat eater)

Jaw of Brontosaurus
(plant eater)

HOW DO WE KNOW ABOUT DINOSAURS?

If no one ever saw a dinosaur, how do we know so much about them? No one lived when dinosaurs lived, so there was no one to write about them. But these ancient animals left records of themselves in the earth. Of course they were not written records, but they can be read just the same if you know how.

Dinosaurs left records by leaving parts of themselves. They left teeth and bones, and scientists have dug up these parts and studied them. They left their footprints, and scientists have found these prints and studied them too.

These things that the animals left are called fossils (fos'-ils). A fossil is something left by a living thing of long ago. Men and women who study these are called scientists (si'-entists), and they are a special kind of scientist called paleontologists (pa'-le-on-tol'-a-jists).

Fossils were made in many different ways. Fossils were sometimes made under water because when dinosaurs died they were often washed into the water of lakes or oceans. They were heavy and settled to the bottom. Mud and clay and sand in the water settled to the bottom too. This covered the animals. The flesh of the animals slowly rotted, but some of the bones did not rot. They stayed in the mud and clay. More mud and clay covered them. It pressed down. A long, long time passed. The bones lay pressed into the clay and sand. The clay and sand slowly turned to rock. Then, of course, the fossils were in the rock.

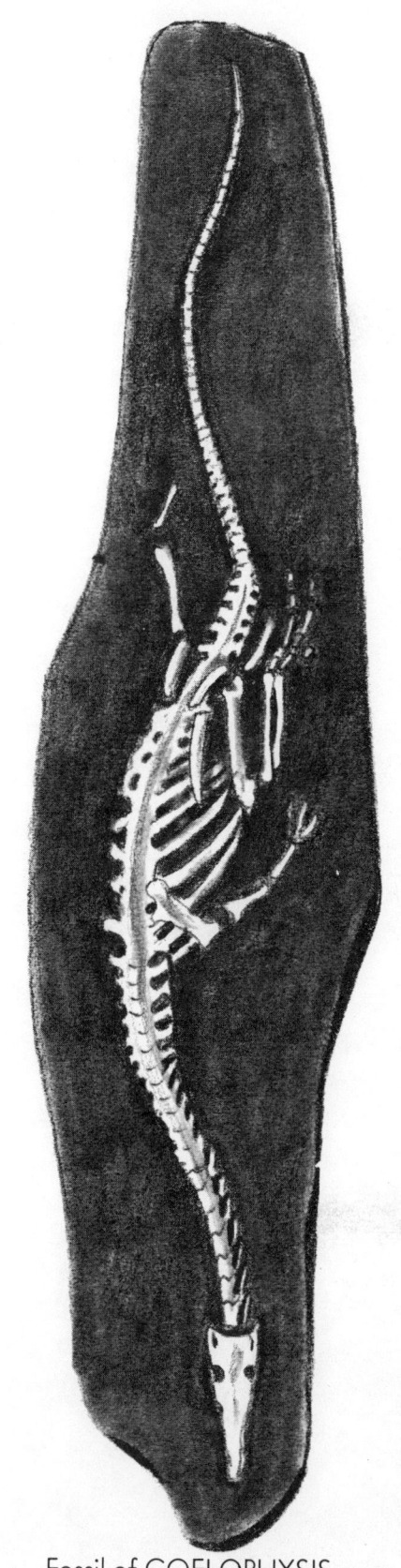

Fossil of COELOPHYSIS

More time passed. The lakes and oceans dried up and then the fossils were on dry land where scientists could dig them up.

Dinosaurs also became fossils when they turned into stone. This also took a long, long time. It happened a little bit at a time. Lime or some other hard material in the water went into the bone and took the place of the material in the bone. When this happens we say that a bone has become petrified (pet′ri-fide).

Fossils were made in other ways too. Sometimes hard parts of the animals made prints of themselves in the soft mud. A dinosaur may have been walking along in the soft mud and left its tracks. Then sand and mud washed into the footprint and kept it from being washed away. Slowly the mud hardened into rock and there was a fossil of the track.

But no matter how the fossil was made, it took a long, long time to make it.

Of course, not all of the dinosaurs that were once alive left their bones. Many of the dinosaurs died on land. Then they rotted and no one ever saw their bones. They did not make any fossils. Not all of the animals that were in the water made fossils either.

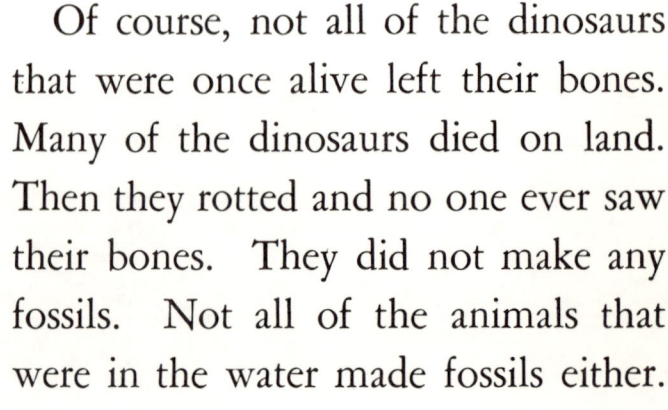

Footprints of dinosaur

But there were enough bones left to tell us a very long story about these animals.

Paleontologists are always on the lookout for these fossils to study them. A paleontologist might be called a scientific detective because he hunts and hunts for facts. Then he puts his facts together and tries to answer such questions as "What did these animals of long ago look like? What did they eat? Why did they disappear?" These are just a few of the problems paleontologists have been trying to find the answers to. A paleontologist collects fossils, he studies them, he thinks about them, he guesses about them

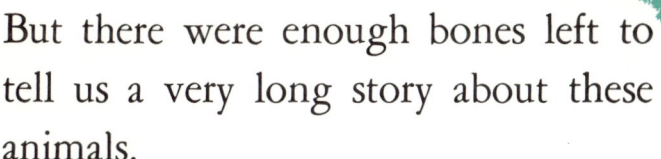

Fossil of ancestor of our crocodile (found in Bavaria, West Germany)

Insect fossil in amber

and then keeps testing his guesses until he is sure he is right. A paleontologist is like other scientists; he makes use of what other paleontologists have discovered. There are still many things that he does not know but he discovers more every day.

But how in the world does such a scientist go about finding fossils so he can answer these questions? It isn't quite as easy as it may sound. He doesn't go out into his back yard and dig a hole and look in it for a dinosaur bone. If he worked this way he would never have discovered the things that you are reading in this book. He first tries to find the place that's *most likely* to have some dinosaur bones in it. And how does he find that? For one thing, he knows what kinds of rocks the bones are usually found in.

A paleontologist knows many things about rocks and how they were made. He is especially interested in the rocks that are made by mud and clay and sand as it settles out of water because they are most likely to have fossils in them.

If you have ever driven through the mountains you have seen that rocks are often in layers like a layer cake. You can see these layers if your road goes through a cut in the mountains, for the layers of rock are often different colors. These layers of rock are not alike. Some are very hard and closely packed together. They were made by great heat down in the earth millions of years ago. They hardly ever have any fossils in them. Some of the rocks are not so hard and not so closely packed together. Some of these are more likely to have fossils in them because they were made when material settled out of water the way mud settles out of muddy water. When this material settled to the bottom it got packed together, and after a long time it turned to stone. Some of these rocks have dinosaur bones in them. So a paleontologist is always on the lookout for rocks like these.

A paleontologist knows a lot about where different kinds of rocks are to be found. When he goes out on a scientific detective trip, he goes where the right kinds of rocks are. Then he begins to look. He may first find a few small bones or teeth or other small fossils. He may only find tiny chips from bones. He may find a part of a bone sticking out of the rock. Then he really begins to do some detective work. He may dig some of the rock away and find that the bone is not so small after all. It may turn out to be a very large bone. It may turn out to be many bones. It may be a whole group of bones that he can fit together and make into an animal frame. This bone frame is called a skeleton (skel′-i-tun). Here in the picture is a skeleton of a dinosaur that was found and

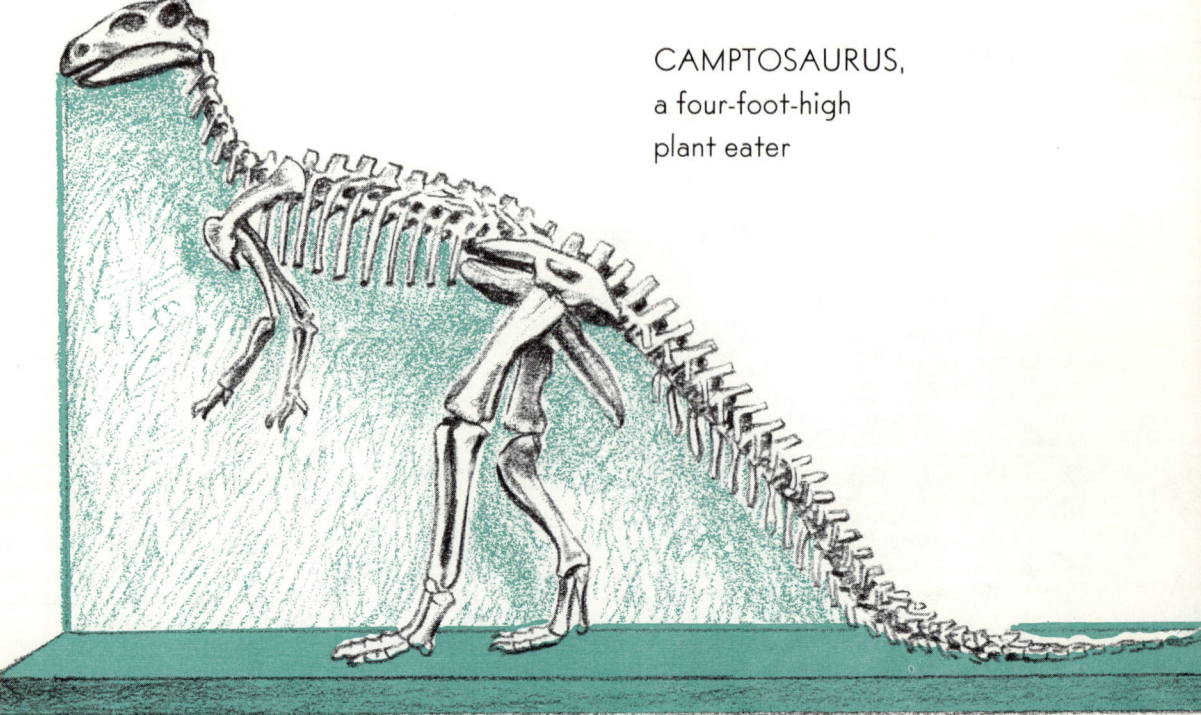

CAMPTOSAURUS,
a four-foot-high
plant eater

put together. Some dinosaur skeletons have been found by paleontologists because they first found very small bones. They then discovered where these tiny bones or pieces of bones came from. Then they found the bones that they put together to make a skeleton.

The scientist may decide to take a big piece of the rock back to his laboratory (lab'-ara-to'-ri); that is the name of the place where scientists work. He digs the rock with the bones in it out of the ground and then gets it ready for the trip to the laboratory.

Digging these bones out of the ground or rock is not an easy job. The scientist can't do it as you would dig out a rock that you wanted to move out of your back yard. You would use a pick and shovel and other large tools. He cannot do this, for he may break the bones in the rocks. He often starts by digging around the rock until he can see the outside of the bones. Then he digs under it very carefully and finally lifts it out.

He can't just dump the fossil rock into the back seat of his automobile and take it to his laboratory. He must be sure that he won't break any of the bones, and they may be as easy to break as a Christmas tree ball. When they are broken they may be useless for study.

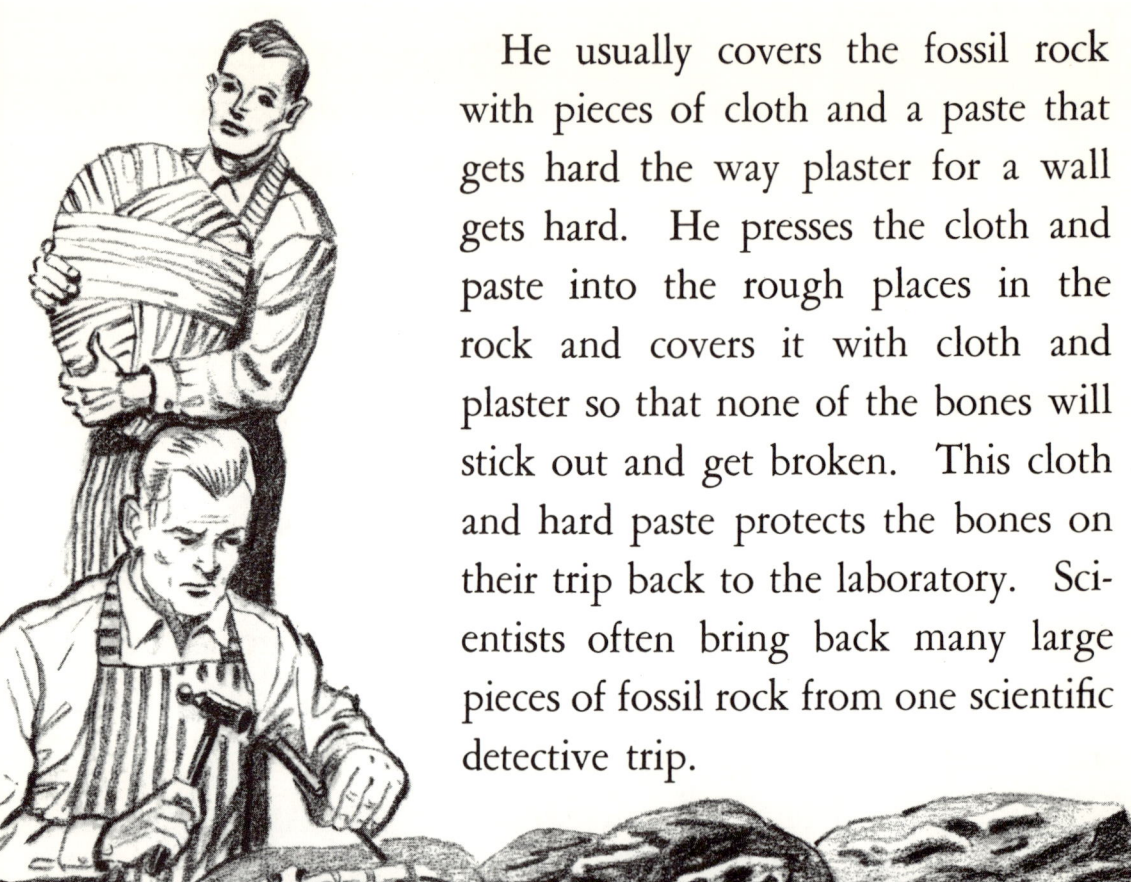

He usually covers the fossil rock with pieces of cloth and a paste that gets hard the way plaster for a wall gets hard. He presses the cloth and paste into the rough places in the rock and covers it with cloth and plaster so that none of the bones will stick out and get broken. This cloth and hard paste protects the bones on their trip back to the laboratory. Scientists often bring back many large pieces of fossil rock from one scientific detective trip.

In the laboratory the scientist begins to chip the rock away from the bones to see what he has really found. On this page is a picture of rock with bones still in it. You can see that it is a long, hard job to get these bones out of the rock. He works very carefully with special tools to get the bones out. Finally he has the many bones in the rock all separated and cleaned up.

Sometimes the bones fit together into a skeleton just as they came from the rock. But often they don't. Then the paleontologist must use everything he knows about animals and bones and fossils to help him make a skeleton.

A paleontologist must know a lot about how bones fit together to make an animal skeleton. He studies skeletons of all kinds of animals. He uses what he knows about bones and skeletons to fit together the bones he has found. He fits the bones together the way you fit the parts of a puzzle together. Sometimes he finds that the bones he has discovered will not make a skeleton at all. But he may discover that some of these bones will fit other bones that he found in another place and has kept. They may not be from the same animal but they may be from the same kind of an animal.

Animal skeletons have been made from bones that came from many different places. Scientists once worked more than fifty years to find the bones to make one skeleton in a museum. They collected the bones from dozens of different places.

If you saved all of the bones of a chicken and tried to put them together to make a skeleton, you would see that it is a very hard job. It is hard to tell how the bones fit together. It is even hard when you know what the skeleton of a chicken looks like. But suppose you had a pile of bones of an animal you had never seen. Then the job would be much harder. Remember that no one has ever seen a live dinosaur, and so the scientist must work very carefully and do plenty of thinking about his bone puzzle. He must work the way you do when you are trying to put together a picture puzzle and you can't find the top of the box with the picture on it.

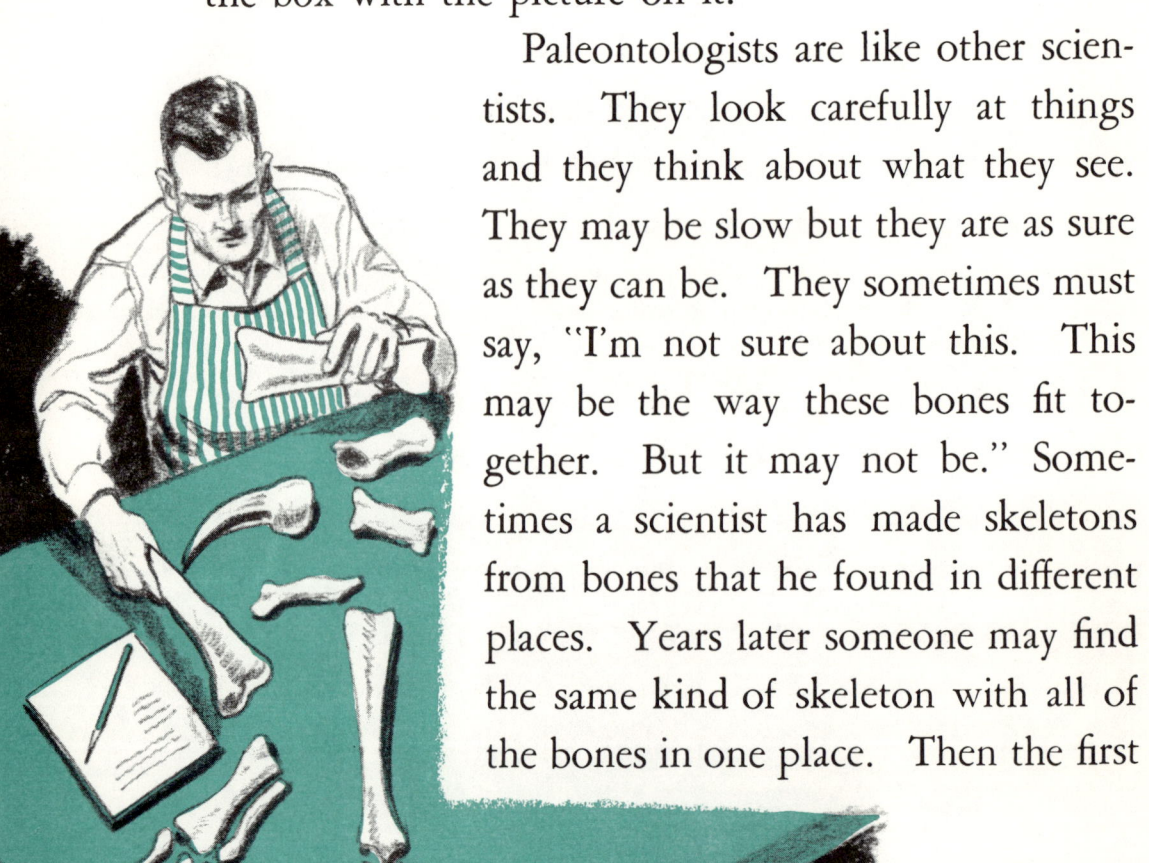

Paleontologists are like other scientists. They look carefully at things and they think about what they see. They may be slow but they are as sure as they can be. They sometimes must say, "I'm not sure about this. This may be the way these bones fit together. But it may not be." Sometimes a scientist has made skeletons from bones that he found in different places. Years later someone may find the same kind of skeleton with all of the bones in one place. Then the first scientist can be sure that his skeleton is correctly put together. But if his skeleton does not look like the new one, it must be changed.

A paleontologist is patient, and it takes lots of patience to look for fossils. Then it takes still more to get them out of the rocks they are in. Then it takes still more to try to fit them together.

A paleontologist is no jumper-to-conclusions. He often says, "Wait a minute now. Let's be sure. Maybe this is true and maybe it is not. Let's get more facts." All scientists must work this way.

One day some scientists were on a fossil-hunting trip and they made a most exciting discovery. They found something that no paleontologist had ever seen before. They were very excited. The picture of what they discovered was in newspapers all over the world. They found fossil dinosaur eggs!

Some of the eggs even had tiny fossil dinosaurs inside them. Scientists studied these eggs and brought them back to learn more about them. Until these eggs were found, scientists were not sure if dinosaurs laid eggs or if their young were born alive.

Even with only fossils to work on, scientists are able to find out many things about the animals from studying their bones. The shape and the size of the bones tell them many things about the shape and size of the flesh that covered the bones when the animals were alive. They can tell about how big and how long the muscles were that moved the bones. When they look at the ends of the bones they can see how they were fastened together. This helps them to see how the skeleton looked. The outsides of the bones often have grooves in them. This helps scientists to see where the nerves and blood vessels were.

Footprints of dinosaurs help scientists tell how the animals walked. They also tell about the weight and the size the walking animal was.

Scientists even use microscopes to get a better look at the bones of the dinosaurs. This helps them to find out more about the animals and what they were really like. Scientists have found prints of the skin of dinosaurs. These prints help them to learn something about the outside of the dinosaurs.

There may be fossils buried in the ground near you. Sometimes when men are digging basements for houses they find them. Sometimes they find fossils in gravel pits or in stone quarries. Sometimes fossils are found when new roads are built. They are sometimes found in the cliffs near the seashore.

The first dinosaur fossils in the United States were found near Philadelphia. They were bones of a duck-billed dinosaur like the one on this page, the Hadrosaurus (Had'-row-saw-rus).

One very interesting place where many dinosaur fossils have been found has been named Dinosaur National Monument, and it is near Jensen, Utah. In this place, scientists have found bones to make twenty-six skeletons, and they are still digging bones out. The skeleton of the Diplodocus (Dip-lod'-o-cus) in the museum in Washington came from Utah. Look on pages 40–41 and you will see what it looks like.

HADROSAURUS

WHATEVER HAPPENED TO ALL THOSE DINOSAURS?

This is a question that is easy to answer. They all died. There's not one left on the earth. They have been dead for millions of years. But when you ask "*Why* did they all die?" you are asking a very hard question. It is such a hard question that the best paleontologists in the world are not sure of the answer. They have ideas that may explain why these large, fierce dinosaurs all died. But no one is sure. Why do *you* suppose they all died? After you have thought about this, read on and see if you have thought of some of the ideas that scientists have thought about.

The first thing to remember is that the climate on the earth has not always been the same. It has

changed from warm to cold and wet to dry and in other ways too. Once the northern part of the United States and all of Canada was covered with ice many feet thick. Once many parts of the United States were covered with water. The earth has changed many times since animals and plants first lived on it.

Many scientists think that these changes in the climate may have caused dinosaurs to die. When the climate changed, many of the plants could no longer live. You remember that many of the dinosaurs ate plants. If the plants were gone their food was gone. Even the dinosaurs who ate animals could not live if many of the plants died. Do you know why? Many of the animals they ate for food lived on plants. Scientists believe that changes in climate may be one of the reasons that dinosaurs died.

DIPLODOCUS in search of plants to eat

But many scientists think there were other reasons why dinosaurs died. Perhaps something happened to their eggs. Maybe some other animals found their eggs and ate so many that there were no more young dinosaurs; or perhaps the change in climate kept the eggs from hatching. Some scientists believe that some dinosaurs may have eaten the eggs of other dinosaurs. But why would this happen all of a sudden? This is a puzzle that scientists have not solved.

OVIRAPTOR
Its fossil skeleton was found on
a pile of dinosaur eggs in Mongolia

Animals must be fitted to live in the place where they live. Most water animals must be able to move about in the water. Water animals usually have fins or flippers or something else to push themselves

36

BRACHIOSAURUS
Some dinosaurs may have died from want of water

through the water. They need gills to breathe under the water unless they stick their heads out to breathe in air. Water animals cannot live on land.

If animals live on land they need legs or something else to move with. They need lungs for breathing. They must be able to protect themselves against their enemies. Land animals cannot live in water.

If the place where animals live changes, then the animals must change too. This takes a long, long time. Animals that live in water cannot suddenly live on land. Perhaps the dinosaurs were not able to change to fit the changes that happened on the surface of the earth. Perhaps that is why they all died. So when the swamps and seas and ponds dried up, the dinosaurs died.

Even though many dinosaurs were very large, many of them had very small heads and almost all of them had very small brains for such large animals. Some scientists think that this may have been one reason that they all died. Their brains were not very good, so perhaps they could not get away from their enemies or protect themselves in other ways. Maybe they just didn't have the brains to stay alive.

These are only some of the possible reasons why dinosaurs died. They may not be the right ones. Scientists are not sure. Perhaps all of the reasons put together could be the right one. Maybe sometime scientists will learn more about why these animals died.

THE AMERICAN MUSEUM OF NATURAL HISTORY
in New York

WHAT CAN YOU SEE IN A MUSEUM?

When you go to a museum you can see many of the things that you have been reading about in this book. Many museums have skeletons of dinosaurs. When you look at a dinosaur skeleton in a museum you will know that once these bones were buried in the earth. Scientists found them, brought them back and put them together.

If you look carefully you can learn many things by looking at a dinosaur skeleton. If you go to the United States National Museum, Smithsonian Institution, Washington, D.C., you will see some very interesting dinosaur skeletons. If you read the labels on them you will discover some very exciting things. On the next page is a label that tells you about the giant dinosaur named Diplodocus that you can see in the Washington museum.

39

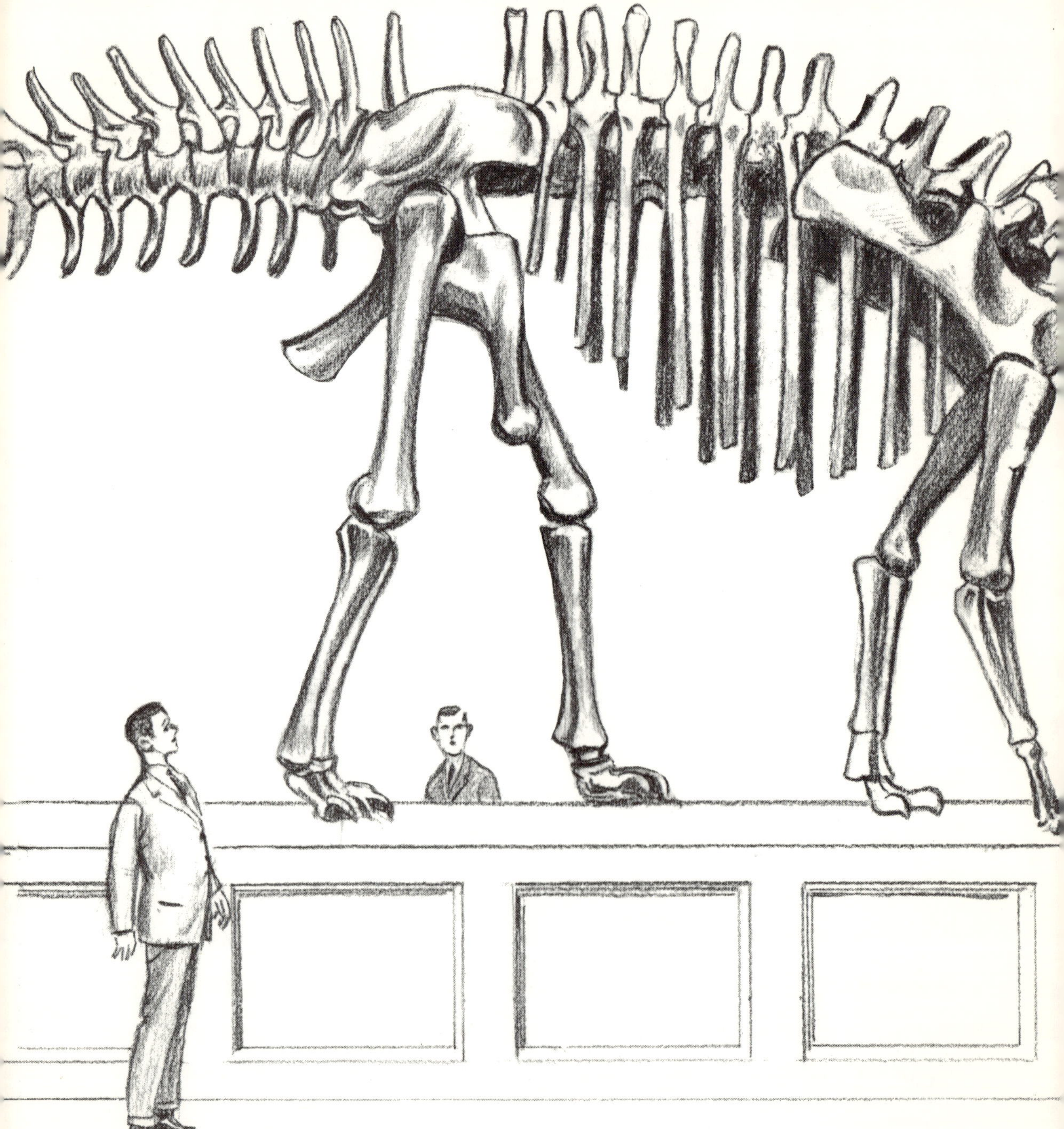

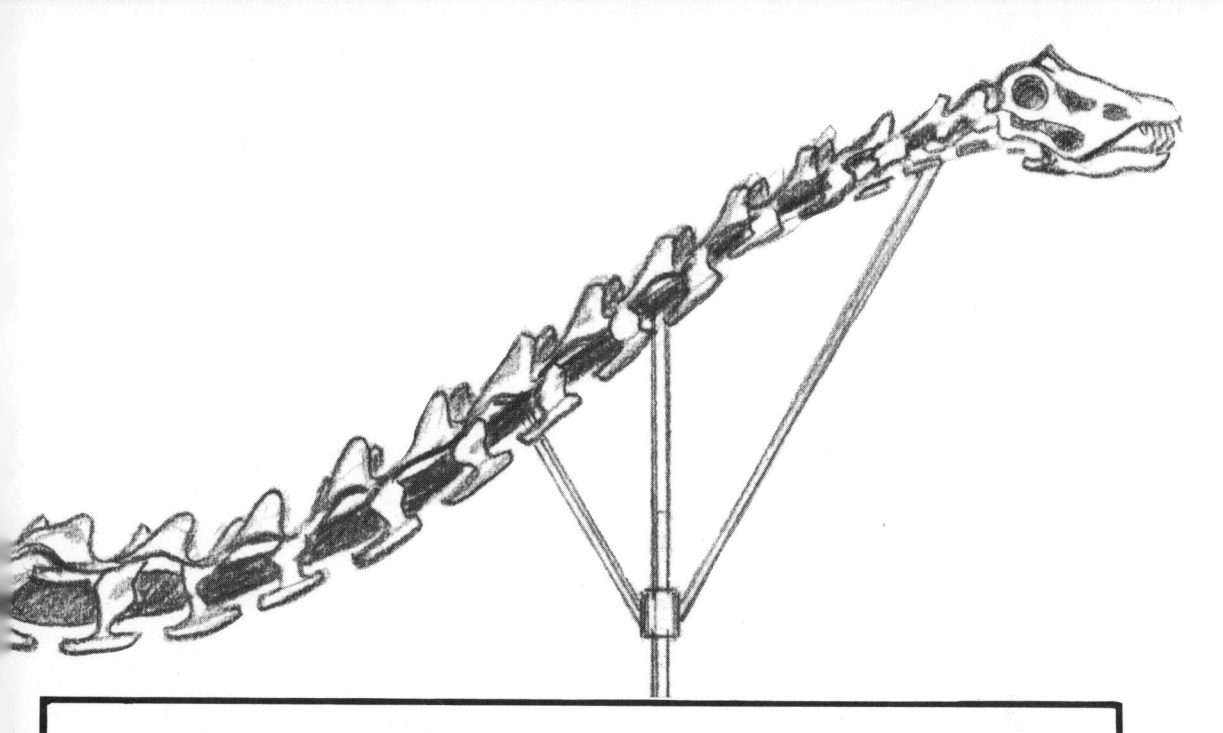

The United States National Museum, Smithsonian Institution, Washington, D.C.

A Giant Dinosaur—Diplodocus
Uinta County, Utah

This skeleton is made from the bones of one animal. The bones were found lying near each other in the ancient sandstone. The parts that were missing have been supplied by plaster casts of actual bones of another skeleton of the same kind of an animal that is in the Carnegie Museum in Pittsburgh, Pennsylvania. These plaster bones are colored so you can tell them from the real bones. This skeleton measures 70 feet, 2 inches long and is 12 feet, 5 inches high at the hips.

Diplodocus was a dinosaur that ate plants. The way its skeleton looks makes scientists believe that it lived in shallow water. This huge animal had a very small skull with weak pencil-like teeth in the front of its mouth. Scientists think that Diplodocus lived on soft, juicy water plants. The neck and tail are long. The tail was especially long, like the tail of some lizards that live today.

You see how much this label tells you? The labels in museums often tell you where the animal lived, what it ate, what size it was and many other things. Here is another label from a dinosaur in the same museum. This label describes an animal that has been restored (re-stored'). It is not just the skeleton of the animal. The animal has been made to look the way scientists think the animal really looked when it was alive. The restored dinosaur looks very fierce and real. On page 42 is a drawing of the dinosaur that has been restored. What does this label tell you?

> The United States National Museum, Smithsonian Institution, Washington, D.C.
>
> ### The Armored Dinosaur—Stegosaurus
>
> The size and general form of this animal are based on bones, plates and spines in our collection here in the museum. From the size and roughness of these plates embedded in the skin it is thought that the skin was thick and wrinkled as shown in this restoration. The color of the animal is our best guess but it is probable that it was dark and about the same over all of the body. The way the huge plates are placed on the back was determined from a skeleton found in the rocks which showed them preserved in this position.

This label tells you how scientists decide what shape and size the dinosaurs probably were. The size and shape of the bones help scientists to know how much flesh covered them. Hollows and humps on the bones help them tell about the animals' flesh too.

Another very exciting place to see dinosaurs is in The American Museum of Natural History in New York City. Here you will see skeletons of many of the biggest dinosaurs and you will see many restorations (res-toe-ra′-shuns) of them. One restoration shows the giant Allosaurus eating part of another giant dinosaur named Brontosaurus. On this page is a drawing of these dinosaurs. If you talk to one of the paleontologists in the museum, he will explain that they are not at all sure that this very Allosaurus ate this particular Brontosaurus, but he will tell you that their skeletons were found near each other so that this may have happened.

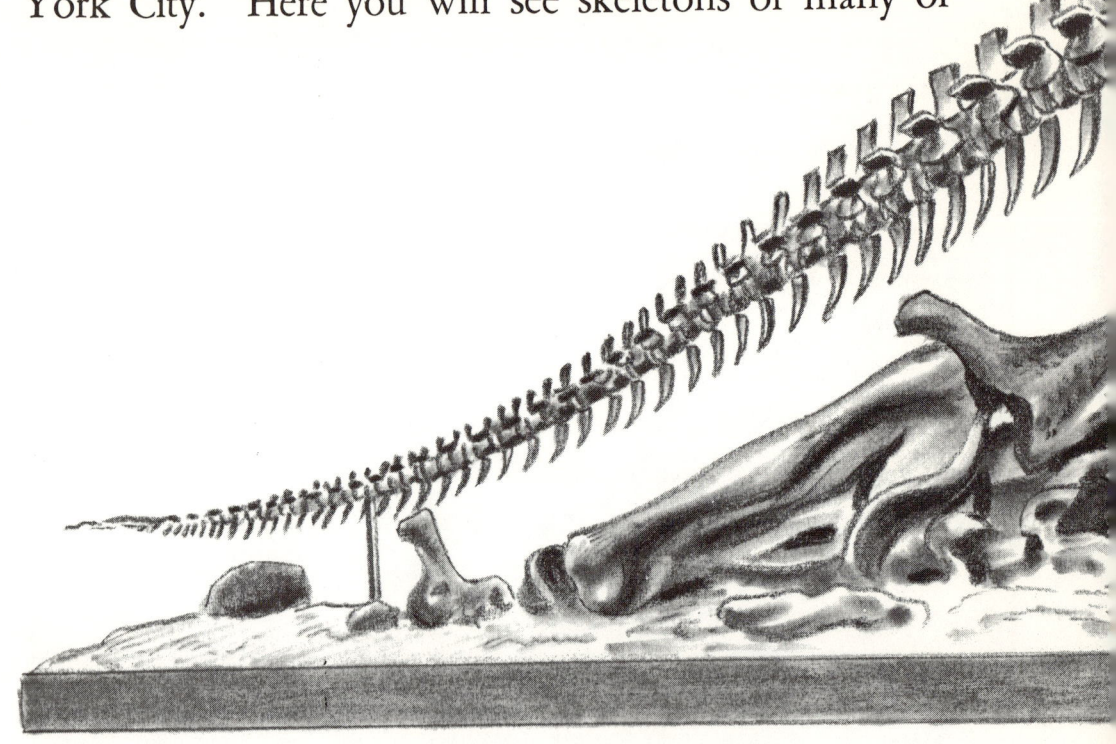

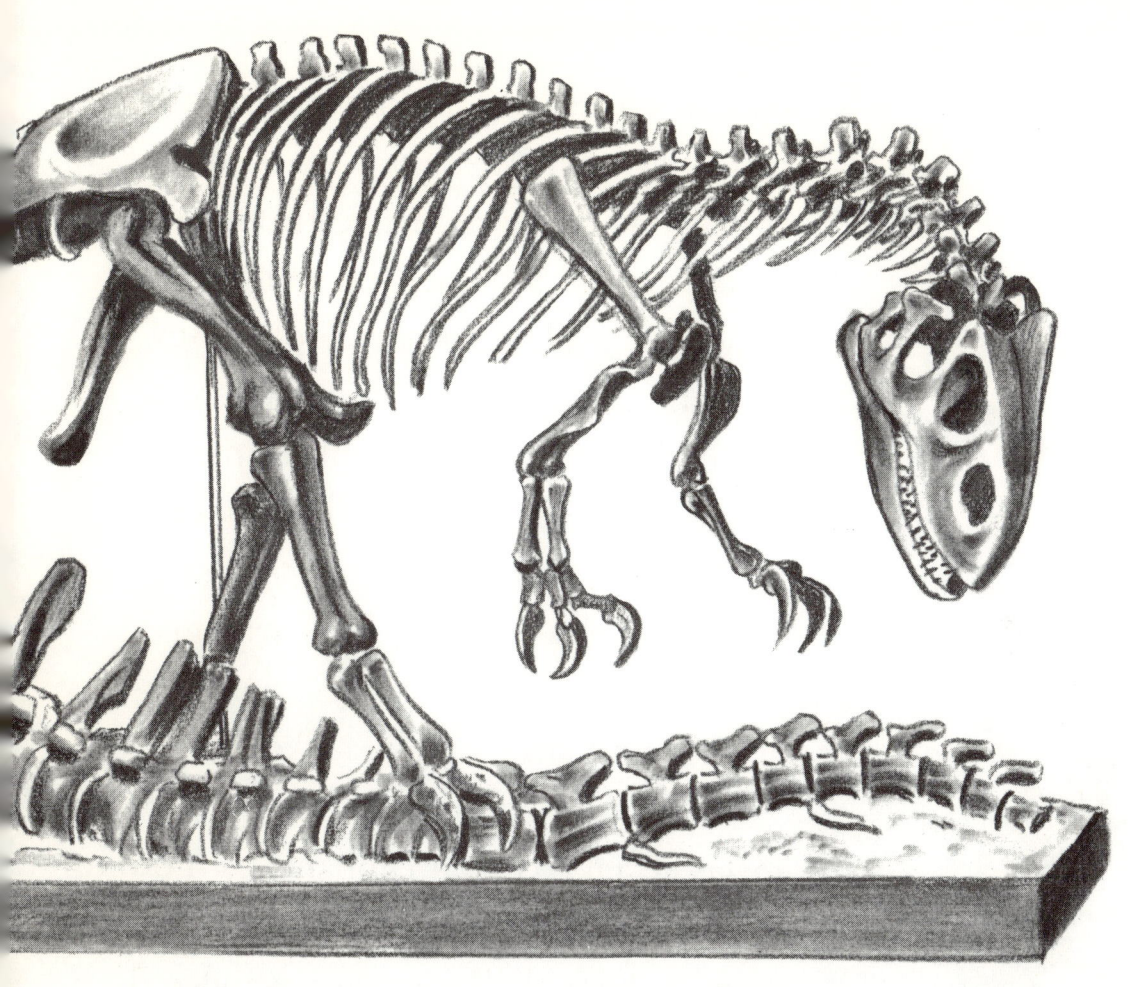

The Chicago Natural History Museum is another good place to see dinosaurs, and so is the Carnegie Museum in Pittsburgh, Pennsylvania and the University of Nebraska Museum at Lincoln, Nebraska. There may be one near you. Even small museums often have dinosaur bones. Many museums have small models that give you a good idea of what these animals looked like. (See page 47)

When you go to a museum see if you can tell which skeleton bones are real and which are plaster. The

45

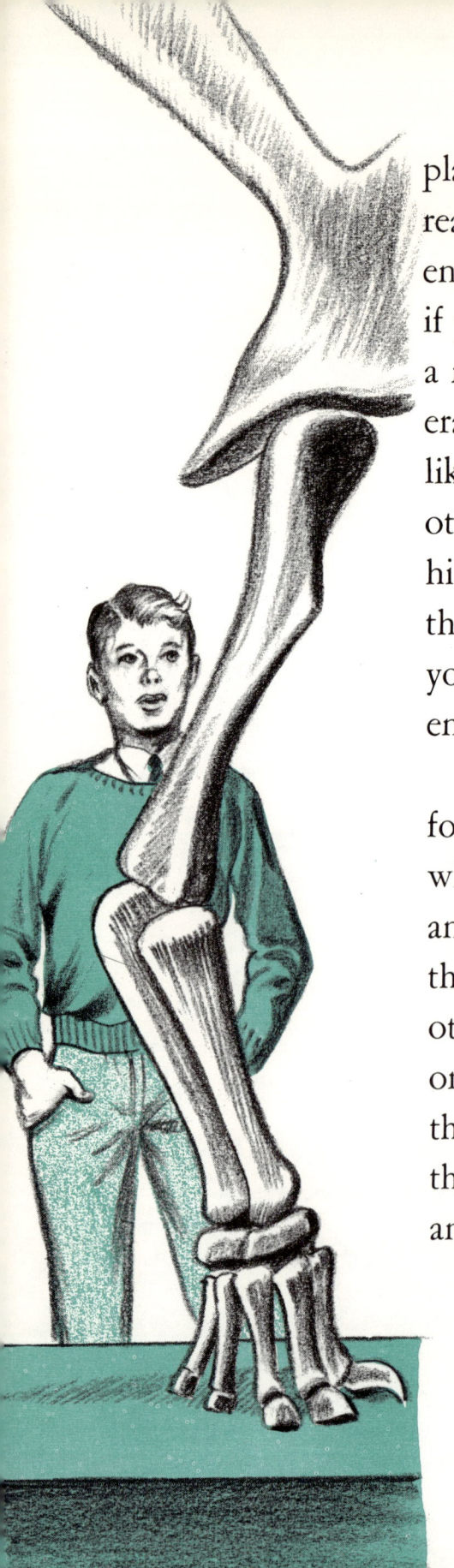

plaster bones are smoother than the real ones and often they are a different color. Look at the teeth and see if you can tell whether the animal was a meat or a plant eater. Look at several animals and see how they were like each other and different from each other. Sometimes you will find an exhibit of bones left in the rock just as they were discovered. This will give you an idea of how much work scientists must do to make a skeleton.

When you go to a museum don't forget to take your imagination. You will need it to imagine what these giant animals looked like as they wandered through the swamps eating plants or other animals, or went to sleep at night, or walked about leaving their tracks in the soft mud of the seashore, or did the other things dinosaurs did millions and millions and millions of years ago.

Some Museums That Have Fossil-Reptile Collections
- Academy of Natural Science, Philadelphia, Pennsylvania
- The American Museum of Natural History, New York, New York
- Carnegie Museum, Pittsburgh, Pennsylvania
- Chicago Natural History Museum, Chicago, Illinois
- Colorado Museum of Natural History, Denver, Colorado
- Geological Museum, University of Utah, Salt Lake City, Utah
- Ghost Ranch Museum, Abiquiu, New Mexico
- Los Angeles County Museum, Los Angeles, California
- Museum of Natural History, University of Oregon, Eugene, Oregon
- Museum of Paleontology, University of California, Berkeley, California
- Museum of Paleontology, University of Michigan, Ann Arbor, Michigan
- Peabody Museum, Yale University, New Haven, Connecticut
- Pratt Museum of Geology, Amherst College, Amherst, Massachusetts
- United States National Museum, Smithsonian Institution, Washington, D.C.
- University of Nebraska Museum, Lincoln, Nebraska
- Webb School of California, Claremont, California

and in Canada:
- Natural History Museum of Canada, Ottawa
- Royal Ontario Museum, Toronto

You will find these dinosaurs in this book

Allosaurus	Al'-o-so'-rus
Brachiosaurus*	Bra'-ki-o-so'-rus
Brontosaurus	Bron'-to-so'-rus
Camptosaurus*	Kamp-to-so'-rus
Coelophysis*	See-lo-fi'-sis
Diplodocus	Dip-lod'-o-cus
Hadrosaurus	Had'-row-saw'-rus
Ichthyosaurus*	Ik'-thi-o-so'-rus
Oviraptor*	O-vee-rap'-tor
Plesiosaurus*	Ple'-si-o-so'-rus
Pteranodon*	Te-ran'-o-don
Stegosaurus	Steg'-o-so'-rus
Struthiomimus*	Stroo'-thi-o-mi'mus
Trachodon*	Trak'-o-don
Tyrannosaurus	Ti-ran'-o-so'-rus

illustration